ISBN-10: 1491085711
ISBN: 978-1491085714

A Few Words

Poetic Reflections on Life

Tanweer Dar

"One merit of poetry few persons will deny: it says more and in fewer words than prose."
~ Voltaire

For Laura: I know how much you like a good quote.

Life is suffering
punctuated by relief.

Thought and feeling,
one without the other
has no meaning.

It is impossible to think another's thoughts.

Nothing is as precious as trust, or so rare.

Those who speak much often say little.

Friendship sustains the soul.

It is tragic that only those who you deeply love can betray you.

Your soul does not exist, but it is the most important part of you.

The word *normal* holds as much meaning as the word *crazy*.

Truth is remarkably
difficult to define.

Many have favourite songs, few have favourite equations.

The songwriter is a
poet who makes
money.

If ignorance is bliss,
then that may explain
why geniuses are prone
to misery and madness.

A philosopher needs a book for that which a poet needs only a line.

What has passed and what is yet to come are separated only by this moment.

Love, not money, is the root of all evil. It is also the root of all good.

There is a direct correlation between how much you say 'thank you' and how happy you are.

Don't be a door mat. Don't be someone who walks all over door mats, either.

Be careful, sometimes
they tell you to stand
up for yourself only so
they can cut you down.

Life or death: which is more terrifying?

There is nothing as beautiful as a sincere, involuntary smile.

The world is round, but you have to go into space to see it that way.

The concept of *owning* land is akin to fleas *owning* a dog.

A million dollars, or a million pounds for that matter, is of little worth to a very thirsty man. He'd much prefer a glass of water.

Rainbows are an effective cure for grumpiness.

All who survive are at once winners and losers.

'For God's sake' is a
truly bizarre expression.

When it is too cold, we wish it to be hot. When it is too hot, we wish it to be cold. When it is mild and between the two, we don't care to notice.

Truly, other animals must consider human beings to be utterly peculiar.

Birds look down on us.
Literally.

Birds are the avengers of Mother Earth. We defecate on her bosom, they defecate on our heads.

Much bad advice is dispensed with good intentions, much good advice with bad ones.

It is dubious that we humans are the most intelligent species on Earth. There is no doubt, however, that we are the most dubious.

Anger should be released productively, not suppressed.

Hate is the same emotion as love, and can be felt just as passionately.

We spill concrete by the tonne over the living Earth and then call dropping a wrapper on it *littering*.

We are wretched, but wonderful too.

Disturbed little men with moustaches have had far too much influence over our history.

Women often get away with things which would land men swiftly in prison.

We are terrifyingly
selfish.

The grass may or may not be greener on the other side, but you won't know unless you take a look.

Loveliness is a quality which makes the heart sing.

Loneliness is a state which empties the heart of song.

The biggest word isn't necessarily the best one.

Politics: the art of talking nonsense and making money out of it.

It is quite possible that the world was more interesting when it was carried on the back of a giant turtle.

Education has limits.
Imagination has none.

Teaching people *how* to think is as much indoctrination as teaching people *what* to think.

I wonder if crabs think laterally... They certainly walk that way.

Trying to discover the meaning of life won't necessarily give your life meaning.

Life is hard. Anyone who tells you otherwise is deceiving you, and themselves.

If the burden is too heavy, the only sensible solution is to put it down. Or, let someone help you carry it...

Human beings are paradoxical by nature: cruel and kind, foolish and intelligent, weak and strong. Is it any wonder we get so messed up?

Honesty is always more helpful than flattery, even if it is not always as welcome.

There are some people in life who are capable of stabbing you in the front *and* the back simultaneously.

Life is as tragic as it is beautiful.

At times life seems much too short, at other times much too long.

There are times to let go and times to hold on tight. Knowing which is which requires extraordinary wisdom.

Forgiving is not forgetting, and forgetting is not forgiving.

People who spend too much time on life's fineries usually miss out on the simple things, which are often more satisfying.

Regretting not having done something feels worse than regretting something you've done.

When it comes to friendship, it is definitely the quality, and not the quantity, of friends that counts.

Poetry makes words
beautiful.

Never underestimate
the power of hugs.

Patience is not always a virtue.

It is truly remarkable, and utterly terrifying, how quickly solid ground can turn into quicksand.

Loneliness isn't a state we suffer; it's merely remembering the fact that we are, ultimately, always alone.

The line between confidence and arrogance is thicker than some would have you believe.

Hope is easily extinguished. It is just as easily kindled.

Silence is often more
deafening then din.

Few things speak to the soul as eloquently as music.

Innocence is a state of mind. So is guilt.

It is not always easy to think for yourself.

Sometimes, people don't notice everything that you do until you stop doing it.

People often believe things which they cannot see and see things which they do not believe.

Trees speak when the wind blows through their leaves.

All of the seasons have their merits, and their drawbacks.

Sometimes people waste their talents, at other times their talents waste them.

Above the clouds the sun always shines.

Keeping your feet on the ground is a bit pointless if you were born to fly.

No one can make your
dreams come true
except you.

Optimism is often unfounded, but very necessary.

Walls are easier to build
than bridges.

It's one thing trying to understand who other people are; it's another thing trying to understand who *you* are.

It is difficult to kindle a fire, but it is even more difficult to put it out once it begins to burn.

Some of the world's
greatest minds did very
badly at school.

We are animals.
We need to be
reminded of the fact
from time to time.

Ants, bees and various other hive insects are far more civilised than we shall ever be.

We think chimpanzees to be very much like us. Indeed, they are. They are violent, cruel and frequently stupid.

Gorillas are smarter, gentler and kinder than chimpanzees. They are also sadder and more endangered.

Human beings are very creative. They are also equally destructive.

The song of the blackbird, though not as famed as that of other birds, is one of the most refreshing celebrations of life.

It would be a tragedy if humanity witnessed the death of Mother Earth. It would be a travesty if humanity survived the death of Mother Earth.

At times, our instincts save us from our intelligence. At other times, our intelligence saves us from our instincts.

We write the future with every breath we take.

Sometimes just breathing is an accomplishment in itself.

Surviving is not the same as *living*.

Pain is tolerable with the knowledge that it will pass.

How can it be that
what we desire is not
good for us, and what
is good for us is not
what we desire?

Words can change minds. Words can change hearts. Words can change history. Words can change the world.

Characters played by actors are, at times, more real than living people in the world.

It is reassuring when a story begins 'Once upon a time…', for there is the expectation that it shall end 'happily ever after'.

A big heart is better than a vast intellect.

The human desire to fly
is closely linked to the
desire to be free.

Big guns make loud noises, but don't always hit the target.

There is nothing quite
like the feeling of
coming home.

Tragedies can be more comical than comedies, and comedies can be more tragic than tragedies.

The tiniest spark can illuminate the darkness.

There is an eternal war being waged between hope and despair on the battlefields of our hearts.

A mid-life crisis doesn't always occur mid-life, nor is it always a crisis.

Being rich is no substitute for being happy.

A problem shared isn't always a problem halved. Sometimes it's a problem doubled.

Life is full of surprises.

There is always more.

It is impossible to justify cruelty.

It is unnecessary to
explain kindness.

You can lose every battle but the last one, and still win the war.

Revenge is frowned upon, but is often deserved and sometimes necessary.

Strength is crying alone in the dark of night and then putting a smile on your face in the morning.

Beautiful souls can be
seen in enchanting eyes.

Sometimes it takes immeasurable courage not to give up. At other times it takes immeasurable courage to give up.

Beauty is anything but
skin deep.

There is nothing in the universe better than a good mother. There is nothing in the universe worse than a bad one.

Take time in your life
to lie back and look up
at the stars.

You never know if
someone loves you. All
you can do is believe
that they do.

Resilience sometimes breeds callousness.

Darkness reigned in the beginning and darkness shall reign at the end, but in between there will have been glorious light.

Thunder scares people, but it is lightning which kills.

If you believe in nothing else, believe in yourself.

The optimist is often disappointed. The pessimist, however, is never happy.

Everyone is pretending.

'I'm fine' is the most common lie told.

We all need to belong somewhere, even if it is to ourselves.

Horses look most beautiful without people on their backs.

Sometimes a beautiful sunrise can herald an ugly day.

The worst lies are the ones we tell ourselves.

A picture can be worth a thousand words, but a word can also be worth a thousand pictures.

Art is the pinnacle of human achievement.

We are all artists,
though we may not
know it.

The importance of being able to express ourselves can never be overstated.

It is extremely difficult, and equally as important, to see the good in people.

The pursuit of happiness should be the most important right we afford to all people, including ourselves.

Those who suffer
more, overcome more.

Sometimes saying
nothing says it all.

An empty heart is a curse like no other.

Nothing is more
necessary than tears.

If we could read others' minds, we would certainly go mad.

Sitting on a park bench
is never a waste of time.

The sounds of nature
possess harmony which
human musicians can
only dream of.

Only you can change
the world you live in.

The only way to find yourself is to express yourself.

Science teaches us *what* we are. Art teaches us *who* we are.

Children *do* know everything: they know how to be happy.

When we grow up, we lose something vital.

The price of
intelligence is insanity.

Love heals the wounds
it has created.

If you give someone more than they can carry, they will drop even that which they can carry.

No one has all the answers.

Our moods are like the weather: ever-changing, unpredictable, visceral.

We are only tempted by what we desire.

Try.

There are daemons in us all, angels too.

Things aren't always as simple as they seem, nor as complicated.

To be inspired is wonderful; to inspire others, more so.

It is said that it is not about the destination, but rather the journey. If it were not for the destination, however, the journey would never have begun.

Some people spend so much time telling others how to live their lives that they forget to live their own.

Those who judge others rarely judge themselves. Those who judge themselves rarely judge others.

Most things which inspire fear also inspire some measure of awe.

Asking *why* can make us thing more deeply. Thinking deeply can make us miserable. Sometimes it's best to just let things be.

Being active is important. Taking a break equally so.

Too much pressure always results in an explosion.

Some things are better
left unsaid.